Acknowledgement

If you are reading this **THANK YOU!!!!**

Your support means everything when it feels like I'm down to nothing. Sometimes, we encounter experiences that break us down past our lowest point. We begin to feel as if nothing can or will help. Then, the faintest cry is answered and a hand comes from that last little glimmer of hope we somehow manage to still hold on to unbeknownst to us. You are that hope!

Cinnamon, Poppa, this is for you.

I have thee most amazing Angels.

Introduction

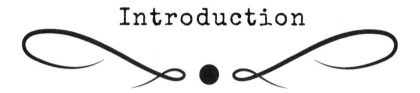

Reflection: not my favorite thing to do. Reflecting reveals hurt, pain, anger and disappointment. All those shoulda, woulda, coulda situations come to light. Sometimes our worst enemy is our mind. The things we tend to focus on. Our negative aspects feed a small mental lizard and build him up to a raging, fire breathing dragon. Once you get to that point of rage and your dragon burns your world to the ground, beautiful flowers begin to grow through the ashes. Your reflecting becomes peaceful. Yes, even in bad situations because if you did what you were thinking instead of what you actually did...you wouldn't be where you are. You are great because you didn't break, you didn't fold, you didn't stop, you didn't let go, you didn't give up. Look at what you've been through, and even in your worst moment- *That,* Yes *that*, didn't stop you because you're here today greater than ever!

Chapter 1

Walking with my roommate to the campus mailbox. The smell of popcorn, students studying and all of the greek(s) out on the yard. It was a private college, but you couldn't tell that to anyone who attended. We were the best of the best, or at least that's what they told us to justify paying this high ass tuition. Can you believe we get fined $10 if we are caught walking on the grass? That was bullshit at its best right there.

My professor couldn't even speak proper sentences, nobody can understand shit she say, but then her ass wanna give a test every week. Why did I even go to college in the first place knowing I didn't want to be here? All my family at home happy-- thinking I'm bout to do something spectacular, they the only reason why I'm not off in some other country wearing a military uniform. My grandma told me off the rip that if I went to any branch she would have a heart attack and die and I wasn't about to see if she was telling the truth or not. Here I am watching Yas, the girl next door drooling over a Que like she never seen a dude before. Ugh, some of these greek(s) made me sick. I just knew that they would prey on a girl like her, long curly natural hair, full lips, 36 DD, flat stomach, with the nice bubble in the back. Only thing is, she would probably have to YouTube how to change a lightbulb or to order take-out over the phone. She was book smart but common sense just wasn't common in her case. She once cut patches in her head cause she heard it makes your hair less thick and easier to comb. She was definitely the ideal chick a guy wanting to hit and run would go for because she would believe just about anything you say. She was beyond gullible. Me and Jay, my roommate were kind of her body guards.

We shut it all down before anyone could exchange numbers. "Yas, come here", Jay yelled --in between KAPPAS party walking on the strip. That was the area right before the student center where our mailboxes were. We went to the mailbox once a week, but had missed a week due to an indoor track meet. Yas came over smiling, hoping we wouldn't walk away before the Ques started hopping. She knew just like clockwork that eventually they would start putting girls on their shoulders and holding them in the air while one of the newbies imitated giving one lucky pick head, and today she hoped it would be her. "Girl I just want Nico to put his face between my legs so I can feel his lips one good time" Yas said, excitedly. For the past two days she had been going on and on about how horny she was and needed some kind of release. Her roommate was gay and whenever she had someone over Yas would come to our room to escape the slurping and moaning sounds. We walked to the mailboxes and decided that we would get the mail and go to the strip to sort it, so Yas wouldn't miss the chance to be teased. The Zetas were party walking and for some reason the newest line of 7 that came out had some dope dances and got the crowd hype. While Jay and Yas were talking I started going through my mail. Pre approved for credit cards, sales papers, a wack letter from the freshman class president reminding us to not drink underage and be responsible, a card from my grandparents, a letter with an illegible name but whoever it was they were locked up. I couldn't think of anyone specific it could be.So much had changed since I was gone. I opened the letter and read the first three lines. Tears instantly streamed down my face and I told my girls i would meet them back at the room. I didn't know if they saw the tears and at this point I didn't care. I tried not to be obvious but I'm almost sure the guy I walked into could tell that I was in a hurry.

I fast paced to my dorm and ran up the three flights of stairs while holding back the urge to cry aloud, screaming frantically. So many questions running through my mind. How did he get my address? What did he know? Just like that the flashbacks began to flow.......Sitting in class waiting for lunch, my stomach was growling and I hoped no one heard it. I read that they had space lunches and pizza today. All I wanted from the space lunch was the Slim Jim's anyway. The pizzas usually tasted like wet dough so I picked the cheese off and the pepperoni and that would hold me until school was over.I would get something to eat from the restaurant I worked at when I got there. I was strongly considering quitting, I get tired of having to wash out the scent of meatballs and cheesesteaks out my clothes and hair. I did like having money though while at school. I was supposed to turn in my rough draft for my graduation project so my teacher could make sure I was on the right track. I had already sent letters requesting informational brochures on cephalopelvic disproportion. I was intrigued but at the same time disgusted by the thought of sex, more or less having a kid at the age of 13. I knew so many people who were already doing it. I didn't hear anything that made me want to try it though.The bell rang and I gathered my belongings for lunch. After I got my food I sat next to my friend Marcie who was focused on seeing what Reek, the new dude was all about. "Girl just look at him, the way he dress...and his lips, mmmmm" She said. "Ok girl, you taking this puberty thing too far" I replied. "I'm just saying, as long as my mom don't find out I'm good" she said with a smile.

We weren't old enough to date but she felt he was at least worth risking her young life to find out cause her mom would kill her if she knew she had anything to do with one of those fresh ass boys, as her mom liked to call them. She carried on about him until lunch was over and with two classes left for the day, the end of school came before I knew it. Marcie and I were outside waiting for the rest of our friends who walked home with us. Once we all got together we were on our usual path. One stop at the store for snacks and then the shortcut through the cemetery. Right before the cemetery Dajah caught up with us so she could walk with Marcus. They had just started going together and Marcus was getting swept off his feet. He was still a virgin but she wasn't. They were walking slightly behind us kissing and she was putting her hand in his pants. Dajah had already knew what to do and how to do it. Marcie noticed that as we walked further through the cemetery they were further behind. "Hold on, lemme go get Marcus before his mom have a fit, you know she be standing at the door waiting on him to get home." Marcie said as she turned back. A few seconds later she returned with the biggest smile on her face, "Yall come here....and be quiet" she oh so loudly whispered while motioning us to follow her. As we followed her we could hear low moans and someone shushing. Of course it was Dajah and Marcus. Marcus was halfway seated on a tombstone and Dajah had her head in his lap, two guesses at what was going on. Marcus then let out an animal like noise that was somewhere in between a yell and cry of distress. Everyone was laughing as they realized the twos' horrible attempt at being discreet.

"Yo who the hell gets head in a cemetery? And who the hell gives head in a cemetery, that's some crazy movie stuff yo" said Sam. He was the oldest of us, but still in the same grade. He almost looked like he was too old to be in high school. Everyone was still in shock whispering about what they had just saw. That was something you don't see everyday and something you don't easily forget. Dajah was wiping her mouth as they caught up with us holding hands. They looked at us and realized they failed horribly at trying to pretend like nothing happened.

Marcus was trying to hide the fact that he was blushing. I bet he was tripping over what just happened in his head too. As we got out of the cemetery and crossed the street, a silver SUV playing " Do something" by Total pulled up. The window cracked and a man yelled "Zee, come here". I looked over to see who was calling me, it was TK, my brothers best friend. I walked over to the car and signaled for my friends to keep walking without me. Marcie flipped me off, I knew she would tell me tomorrow about how I left her stuck with everyone else for the rest of the walk home. "Wassup?" I said with a smile. "Get in, I will drop you off at work." he said.

TK and my brother had been friends since they were born, he was practically like a brother. His mom and my mom went to elementary school and grew up together, then his mom moved away for a few years but still kept in touch and visited. Our moms ended up pregnant around the same time, causing them to grow closer. They moved within an hour of each other and the rest was history. TK was a few months older than my brother, and they both were 7 years older than me. His mom had 6 kids, my mom had 4.

As we were driving, TK was not on the usual route to my job so I looked over at him to see what was going on. He was blasting Biggie- *"Would You Die For Me"*, moving his shoulders to the beat and looking at his pager. He then looked up and said, "Hold on, I gotta get something from my homie." He turned down a side street, pulled over and hopped out the car. He walked to the house on the corner and a guy met him at the door. They dapped each other up and he went into the house. I just sat there looking around and thinking about what I saw during the walk. *I couldn't believe how bold Dajah was.* In elementary school, hell just last year she was so quiet and reserved, you almost had to force her to talk. She would walk with her head down not making eye contact and you almost didn't know she was there unless you heard her unique laugh. I wondered what happened between then and now that had changed her. Around five minutes later he returned and walked abruptly to the car and got in. "Oh now he wanna act like he in a rush? I thought. "You ready to go to work youngin'?" He asked. As he swung the door open and hopped in with a smile. I quickly nodded, "just ready to get there." As I looked at him I noticed traces of white powder on his upper lip and his nose slightly running. I could feel myself frowning with my lip up in disgust. I was never good at hiding my facial expressions. To ease my look, I pointed to his face and he wiped without hesitation. "Don't worry, I was just testing the product" he said, adding "chill, it's not that deep". At that moment I knew he saw the look on my face. Oh well, he should be used to it by now. He's gotten this look from me a time or two before. I turned and looked out the window. I knew there was no need for me to even express how I felt so I didn't bother. It's not like he would even listen to me anyway.

Chapter 2

The rest of the trip we rode in silence. Pulling up to my job he asked if I needed a ride home, I told him I would page him if I did. My mother had her hands full with my little brothers so she would usually send my older brother. He talked trash but he was happy to get out the house. Whenever my brother picked me up, he always had snacks and a horror story about when he used to work at a restaurant. That became our thing and I looked forward to it. It was the perfect thing to help me unwind, especially when my day went mad long and customers or school irritated me.TK watched me get out of the car and this time it felt weird, I could actually feel his gaze upon my back. I tried my best not to turn around as I walked into the building so I focused on the old tattered menu hanging near the front door. I clocked in and went straight to work hoping today wasn't exhausting. It was a normal day, the customers came at a steady pace, mostly spread out. I began cleaning part of my nightly duties in between customers so I wouldn't be there so long after closing. My brother taught me that and I was so glad he did. I probably would have discovered this eventually, but I was the type to ask if it was okay first instead of just doing it. During my lunch break I called home to see if my brother would be coming to pick me up, the phone rang with no answer. I then paged him with our special code 1455 4013. If you looked at it on his pager it almost said ASSHOLE. I knew it would get a rise out of him. We often terrorized each other while mom was at work. I sat and waited for his call. My wings I ordered were ready and he had until I was finished them to call me back, but nothing. My break was over and I went back to work. The girl who handles To-Go orders came up to me as I was taking an order. She handed me a slip of paper that said TK will pick you up.

I handed the table's order to the kitchen and threw the other slip into the trash. I could still smell the grape scented ink from her gel pen as I walked away. The tables were steady and the tips were normal. It was more money than what I had so it was cool. As the night ended and I was finishing up my cleaning, I recognized TK's car approaching. If I couldn't see his car, I still knew it was him the way *"Kissing You"* by Total was blasting. I didn't know of anyone else who loved Total the way he did. He knew the songs the radio played and the songs most people never heard of. He had the cassettes and CD's, he for sure was one of their biggest fans. I got into the car and was immediately entertained by his horrible high pitched voice-overs to the song. He was rocking with hand movements and even used a can for a microphone. This was more than a drive home, this man was in full concert while floating through the streets. His smile was so bright and he was all in to what he was singing. He sung every word, adlib and even knew when the beat was changing throughout the entire thing. *"Kissing You"* went off and was followed by Hi Five *"I Like The Way,"* as soon as the beat dropped the concert continued. As he sang." *Cause When I'm With You- You're such a Good Time*" He pulled the car over and looked at me. "You know what I wonder?" He said. I shook my head *no* and looked confused. "You got a lil' boyfriend or something?" He asked. Again I shook my head *no*. Why was he asking me this and why would that be something he was wondering? He got out the car and walked around to my side. As he opened the door he reached for my hand. Not knowing what his intentions were I let him grab my hand to see what all this was about. He rubbed my hand on the seat of his pants as I noticed they were unzipped and I then felt the warmth from his erect penis on the palm of my hand.

I froze as my heart raced. He moved my hand in a circular motion and was trying to get me to grab it. I quickly closed my eyes, afraid to look down and see what I already knew I was feeling. I had never felt anything like this before. What was I supposed to say or do? My palms began to sweat. Before I could say anything he was grabbing my face and putting his tongue in my mouth. I felt his thumbnail in my cheek. I slowly tried to move my hand back without him noticing. His lips were soft and kind of pleasant but I didn't want my first kiss to be with the guy who was like a brother to me. Ugh. Now I'm disgusted. Despite all my thoughts, all I managed to say was " This is weird" while still attempting to pull my hand back and put it in my lap. He looked at me. His eyebrows scrunched and he got offended. "What the fuck you mean this weird? Why you acting like I'm some random?" " I knew you before you knew yourself so who better to teach you than me?" He said angrily. Confused and afraid I stared at him, not knowing what to say. I wiped my lip and soon realized that was a mistake."You know what, I got something for ya lil ass" he said. He grabbed me by my neck with one hand and put his penis in my mouth with the other. I tried to close my mouth but his grip on my neck grew tighter. As I began to choke he forcefully pushed himself deeper into my mouth. There was no room to go further but he still pushed. I could feel him in the back of my mouth as thick, slow moving spit began to gather and slowly trickle down my throat. I wanted to spit so bad. A snot like string went from my throat to my tongue. It reminded me of a slimy spider web. The thought creeped me out. My eyes watered and I gagged. My mouth filled with saliva and I resisted the urge to throw up, I could taste those wings again. He again tightened his grip, causing me to see the glittery version of tv static in my sight. He was actually getting excited watching me.

As he began to thrust harder and faster, the corners of my mouth stretched and split. My jaw was aching and began to shake. I had never had my mouth open this wide before. I could taste the blood as I felt the corners stinging. The glitter got brighter and began to dance around. TK kept going. I dug my nails into his sides so he would stop but he liked it. My nails in his skin only encouraged him. He adjusted his fingers and tightened his grip. While he continued to thrust, the pain in my mouth and neck grew. It felt as if I could feel my blood pumping in my neck veins. I opened my watering eyes hoping he would see me and end this. He was biting his lip with pleasure. He grabbed my hair with his free hand and pushed my head into his waist. I could taste the saltiness of his semen as he released it into my mouth As I gagged he pulled back, letting the remainder of it go on my face. I fell forward, throwing up regurgitating remnants of chicken wings and semen as I drifted off. All I wanted to do was breathe. Unable to fight off the 6'2", 220 pound man who "knew me before I knew myself". All I could hear in my head was the song lyrics " *I Like, The Way, You Kiss Me --when we're playing the kissing game* " as visions of him kissing me replayed in my head in slow motion. This was like a bad nightmare that I couldn't wake up from. As I came to, all I could do was cry. I was still riding in the car with this guy who I just found out I really didn't know at all. Why would he do this to me? All these years he's been around my family. Was this what he's been wanting to do to me all along? Afraid to look around and see where I was, I touched my sore neck and put my tongue in the corners of my mouth to see if I was still bleeding, I tasted blood and semen. How disgusting. My mouth watered as I fought the urge to throw up again. Apparently I hadn't been out long, as my face was sticky and there was still semen on it. I wiped my mouth and face using my shirt. I really couldn't believe his ass just did that to me and left me in the seat like I was nothing. Then he had the nerve to get in the car like nothing happened. This can't be real.

This had to be some kind of messed up dream. My vision was still a little blurry and maybe I had slight contact from the blunt he was smoking but either way I wanted to be anywhere but where I was. We pulled up to my house and I began to reach for the door to run out the car. He hit the button on the drivers door to ensure it was locked and turned towards me while throwing money in my lap. "Yo, you my shorty now and I want you to know that I got you." He said with a smile. He looked at me while biting his lip. I was terrified, this isn't the way I wanted to start liking boys and I certainly didn't want it to be him. "Oh, if you decide to share our encounter I need you to know that I'm willing to make sure whoever you tell goes away for a long time. We don't need any negativity, he said as he flashed a bag of coke. I'm not quite sure what that meant but I wanted out the car ASAP. This day couldn't be any worse. I rushed into the house and threw my book bag down while heading straight to the bathroom. I wished I could bleach the entire day away. I turned the water as hot as it could go and was prepared to melt my skin if possible. I took my clothes off, not ever wanting to see my shirt again. I could just buy another work shirt. It even had small traces of vomit on it. I lathered my hands with Ambi soap and began applying it onto my face heavily. My entire face was white and I could see slight bruising on my neck, it was sore to the touch. I looked in the drawer at the sink to find something soothing to put on my lips. I found Peroxide and Carmex. The bubbling from the peroxide was somewhat soothing in a weird way. Now the Carmex, it stung like crazy. No time to focus on that, I hopped in the shower and slid to the bottom. I loved the way the hot water felt, like each drop was grabbing on to a bit of shame and dragging it down my body to take it down the drain. I know the shower wouldn't make me feel whole again but it felt good to dream after a night like this.

I wanted to tell my brother, my mother, somebody. Not at the risk of having something done to them though. I loved my family and couldn't imagine not being able to be with them because of something that I did. How could I begin to prove that this happened? How could I even say what happened to me out loud? I was ashamed and embarrassed. I can't believe I was actually forced to give someone head. That was beyond disgusting! I don't see how people even enjoy that.

As I slept, my mind kept replaying the events and I tossed and turned all night. I couldn't get comfortable, couldn't have peaceful dreams, my whole mental state was all over the place. Hopefully being around everyone at school would take my mind off things. I didn't have to work so that was good, I had to buy a new shirt.

Marcie met me on the corner like always and we waited for the others to show up. "So it's a lil early for hoodie season don't you think?" she said sarcastically. "Yeah I know but I gotta do laundry" I said with a weak smile. I was hoping she didn't catch my lie, I just had to cover my bruises up. I hated to have a secret this big and couldn't tell her. She was my best friend and it killed me to keep this in. "Is TK picking you up again?" she asked. Ugh don't say that name I thought as I shrugged my shoulders. "What we eating? I got lunch money, whatever you want I got you" I said as she smiled super hard. "This must be my lucky day" she said. Really I just wanted to change the subject so I wouldn't hear that name again.

The others met up with us and we walked to school. After the first bell rang, Marcie ran up to me super excited....."Girl! Reek wanna go to the party with me this weekend, you still going with me right?" She asked. I could care less about this party I thought. "I guess so, I will let you know for sure" I replied. I couldn't focus on anything, my mind was all over the place. The rest of the day was filled with practice for my presentation at the end of the week. I focused on that so my mind was occupied.

Who would have known that Cephalopelvic disproportion could be linked to so many other health issues. I was alarmed but intrigued to learn about Africa and other countries that had high case numbers due to young women getting married to grown men and trying to birth kids while they were still not fully developed kids themselves.

Young girls varying in ages sometimes younger than 14 would marry older men who would present items to gain approval from her parents. In order to earn this approval, the men would gift the family with livestock and other forms of wealth. The family would have celebrations and show off their gifts, not truly knowing what was awaiting these little girls. These young women would get pregnant and since their bodies weren't fully developed, the baby's head would be too big to push out and they would often get stuck. Due to lack of resources and under developed medical facilities, the babies would sometimes die and have to be removed in pieces. Some would be born with birth defects and the women would be faced with a number of complications, often unable to afford medical procedures. In some cases, the husbands would disown their wives, sending them back to their parents or out to fend for themselves. A number of women would end up with more complicated issues such as an Obstetric Fistula. This would cause the women to constantly leak urine, feces, or both.

The presentation was for public speaking, but also had to have 5 pages with 1 resource page. Each task was a portion of the grade. If this was what college was like just count me out. This made my head hurt. Writing this paper and talking about it made me feel smart, but I wasn't about to spend 8 years in college to be a doctor-- NOT.

The week flew by entirely fast, before I knew it --the day was Friday. Man, between work and this presentation I barely had time for anything else. That was a good thing. At the end of class, I went to pay my class dues. Mr. Simpson, the accountant informed me that my dues were paid and I had excess on my account. Where did this come from? I know I didn't give them the money and my parents were not the type to do so either. I could only think of one other person and I don't want to be right. Just the thought of seeing him again made my skin crawl. It's already taking a lot out of me to pretend to be normal.

Luckily I had a best friend who was a great distraction. Marcie was a big ball of energy today and it was keeping my mind off everything else. She was super excited about the party tonight. Yes, she convinced me to go. I was trying to stay occupied physically and mentally. Our walk home was filled with outfit possibilities and what if scenarios. Marcie even entertained the thought of her dancing and ending the night with a kiss. I wish I was as excited as her, kinda. My thoughts were then interrupted by the sounds of giggling and moaning. Dajah and Marcus.....again. I don't know why the hell these two get off on doing stuff in the cemetery, it would creep normal people out. This time, Marcus had his hand in her pants and she had her hand in his. I guess it was a lot of good yanking and poking from the way they sound. I didn't wanna think about anything involving a boy doing anything. This time I wasn't waiting, let them have fun. Everyone else was entertained, I kept walking. I went into the corner store to get a sandwich and some snacks. I walked down the aisle to the cooler to get a drink. "Excuse me" said Malik. He went to the school near mine, we always saw each other in passing and knew the same people but never really spoke enough to hang out. From the handful of words we ever exchanged, he seemed cool. I looked back as I moved out the way. He smiled and so did I. I got my sandwich and paid for everything. As I was leaving the store he was walking out behind me. "Hey, do you mind if I walk with you?"He asked. "Sure, no problem" I said. We walked the 4 or so blocks and talked about school, work, and the party. Turns out he was going to the party also. He was going cause his friend didn't want to go alone and he was looking forward to seeing me there. Now I gotta change my outfit choice. I gotta wear something cuter. We had a good conversation. It was nice to have a normal but distracting conversation. As we parted ways, I was replaying our conversation. I was walking alone, happy with a smile.

While turning the corner, a car approached speeding up. The windows were tinted so I couldn't see into the car. The driver pulled onto the curb, slammed the car in park and hopped out. It was TK. My smile quickly faded. "Baby tell me you not cheating on me, I saw you walking with that bum ass dude." He said as I stared at him in shock. "After all we been through this how you do? I thought we had something special, don't I mean more to you?" He asked while walking towards me. He backed me up against the wall and put his head on mine. "I'm not jealous or nothing cause I know they ain't got nothing on me baby. In fact, Look what I had for you" he whispered as he rubbed his penis on my hand. "Nobody can give you what I can, and you know it. I won't let nobody take you away from me." He said, as he began to breathe heavily. He continued to rub his penis on me, going from my hand to my side and my thigh. It was clear that he was aroused. He was breathing heavy, panting. His eyes were red. Maybe he was high. He attempted to kiss on my neck, but I moved my head. He took the palm of his hand and pushed my head against the wall, still rubbing up against me. "You know what, you don't even deserve this right now, I'd rather you beg for it and I should make you but this isn't the place." he said as he pulled his shirt over his penis and got back in the car. I was confused. Hesitant to move in case he came back.Sadly that wasn't the weirdest thing I've ever had him do or say. I rubbed my head where it hit the wall, it was a little sore but not too bad. It would definitely be a little knot. Surely my life had to be more than pop up harassment by my older brothers best friend. I don't even know how I ended up in this situation. This wasn't the TK I knew at all. I've never seen him act like this or even be aggressive. Maybe it was from testing his product or whatever he wanted to call it. Could he be taking it instead of just smoking weed? Why am I even thinking about why he's doing this? Wrong is wrong. Ok girl try to act normal and focus on the party I told myself.

After getting dressed, I met up with Marcie. We got some quick food so we wouldn't be hungry at the party. I don't eat everybody food and I didn't know who cooked what. To be on the safe side I ate before I went and left nothing to the imagination. Shit knowing my luck lately some crazy stuff would happen to me if I did eat mystery food. I'm not about to set myself up like that. Plus I had someone who wanted to see me there.

It was a good crowd when we got there, not too many people. There was still enough room so that you could comfortably walk through. That wouldn't last long though. Basement parties were always lit, the walls would be sweating in no time. Wait til they start playing the reggae.

People start coming out of nowhere to find somebody to grind on. It was about to be *Saucony, Air Forces and Shell Toes* everywhere. Once I started dancing, I stayed on the dance floor til it was time to leave. I loved to dance, music took my mind off everything. I knew by the end of the night my shirt would be soaked and my hair and face would sweat. I learned my lesson from the last party and knew this time to wear dark colors. I was not trying to have another outfit ruined. If someone bought a fresh pair of jeans, popped the tags off and wore them without them being washed first, they were sure to rub dye on someone else's clothes during dancing.

I had a perfect light blue v cut shirt that tied in the back but had just enough fabric to cover everything. It fell nicely upon my lower back so that it accented the little bit of shape I thought I had. It was not the best decision to wear it to a party because once that dark blue dye got rubbed on the bottom of it, no amount of treating/ washing got it out. Sadly I can't find another shirt like it anywhere.

I was standing next to Marcie waiting on a good dancing song to play when I felt a tap on my shoulder. It was Malik. I looked at him and smiled. He smiled back and grabbed my hand. We walked over near the corner where you could kind of hear. "I know you out with your girl but save a dance for me if you can" he said into my ear. I nodded. I went back over to Marcie who couldn't wait to ask me what was going on. "Girl he fine" she said excitedly. "Speaking of fine, where is Reek?" She asked as she scanned the room. "If he don't show up, oh well.

I see another cutie I wouldn't mind dancing with" I knew by her comment she was ready to hit the dance floor and so was I. People were starting to pour in and there would be no elbow room shortly. The music was loud, vibes were good, and the smell of spritz was in the air. Ponytails and edges were sweating out, it was a great time. Just when we were about to take a break, Luke-Scarred came on and everyone was gettin in position as "Cap D Coming" began to repeat. All the girls ran to the middle and all the guys were either behind a girl, or looking to see who was dancing. The girls couldn't wait to put their hands on their knees.

This was the perfect opportunity for anyone who had their eye on someone to make a move and it was happening left and right. Marcie and I were dancing with each other, having a great time. Reek came up behind her and I was suddenly party of one. I didn't mind, I'd much rather dance alone. She had been waiting for him anyways. As the song went off, I went outside to get some air. It was muggy in there from all the sweat and teenage hormones raging. I tried to lift my shirt just a little so that I can feel the air on my skin. My actions were cut short by Malik. He placed his hand on mine and ever so smoothly reminded me that no one needed to see my skin, especially since he "wanted me to himself" If he only knew what my life had been like recently. He probably wouldn't even want to speak to me.

Those words were normally alarming seeing as how I just experienced some crazy stuff, but I didn't feel that way when he said them. They came off as subtle and comforting, like I could trust him. I should be guarded cause I don't really know him. I was all types of confused. Although, this did feel like a nice break that I needed. Maybe all dudes weren't complete dummies. He left a little hope lingering. I entertained the conversation and even the thought, though I would never tell him that. He was nice to talk to. We held hands and continued to talk, we walked down the street to get away from the music and people.

Chapter 3

He told me how he noticed me a long time ago and had always wanted to find the right moment to approach me. He was slightly intimidated by Marcie because she was so forward and out spoken. He said he thought that if she was around, he wouldn't stand a chance. He's obviously thought way too much about this lol. "So tell me something" he said as he looked me in my eyes. I smiled. As I looked back into his, a shadow rapidly passed causing me to turn my head. The moment I did, TK was punching Malik in the face. Malik bent over grabbing his jaw in shock, still trying to figure out what had happened. TK grabbed my arm tightly and pulled me to his car. He was enraged. "I told you nobody taking you from me and I meant that shit. I thought I made myself clear but I see you still need some convincing. "You mine and everybody better fucking know" he ranted. He slammed the door and drove off angrily. His tires screeched and you could smell the rubber. He was driving through the streets aggressively, barely stopping for red lights. He zipped between cars and stared at drivers angrily in passing. We went to a strange looking three story house, with a weird shaped awning. He hopped out and slammed the door. He walked to my side, snatched the door open and grabbed my arm. "Come on" he demanded. I hesitantly walked with him into the house. He was pulling me. We went to a small room on the right that had little to nothing in it. There was a TV and mattress on the floor. It looked like a crash spot. "Wait right here" he said as he left out closing the door. All that went through my head was --what the hell? Where was I and what was he about to do this time? He came back in the room, rubbing his nose. He sat down next to me and looked at me angrily. "Look man, I don't mean to be like this, I just get frustrated. You my girl and I try to show you that I care but it seems like you can't see that we are meant to be together. I didn't wanna hit dude. "But it looked like he was about to kiss you or something and I can't have that". He then pushed me back and began to kiss on me.

"TK, stop. This isn't right. This isn't supposed to happen. Just take me home and I won't say anything, I promise, I told him --as I was trying to sit up. He shook his head *no*, and put a finger to my lips telling me to be quiet. He placed his hand in the middle of my chest, pushing me back and not allowing me to sit up. I grabbed his hand, he looked at me with an irritated face and punched me. My head fell back and I was dazed. It wasn't a knock out punch, but just hard enough to let me know that he was in control and I should do as he says. He climbed on top of me and lift my shirt, licking the barely A cups I had. As I began to squirm he smiled, pushing his hands down on my shoulders. I was still kind of dizzy. He took one hand and unfastened my pants. I began to cry, I was hoping what I thought was not about to happen. "Please don't do this" I asked. "This is not you, this is not what you want, please don't." I begged. He put his hand on my neck and slightly applied pressure, shushing me. I closed my eyes making a horrible attempt to prepare myself. He pulled my pants down, rubbing his hands over my panties. He smiled and told me that everything would be okay. He asked me if I trust him, I shook my head no. He grabbed my panties and pulled them to the side. While letting out a low moan, he rubbed his finger around the outer lips of my vagina. He inserted it slightly and paused. "Damn this shit feel good, I gotta see how you taste" he whispered as he removed his finger and put it in his mouth. He drug his tongue across his top lip and lowered himself towards my waistline. He began kissing me slowly from my waistline to the opening of my vaginal lips. He moved his tongue in and out and up and down. He gripped my thighs and pulled me closer to him, applying more pressure with his tongue. As horrified as I was to move, there was a sensual feeling I had never felt before. Was it sick that I was kind of enjoying the feeling? I mean this wasn't supposed to be happening at all but it did feel kinda good. Why was I getting turned on?

I laid there in a daze, trying to figure out how to end these sick encounters. I just wanted to be a normal teenager. My mind was racing a million miles a minute. I didn't have a solution, but I was determined to find one. I was so deep in thought that I hadn't noticed that he left the room. He came back with a towel and wiped me. Then he told me to put my pants on because we had to go so that he could make some money. I couldn't look at him, I hated every fiber of his being at this point. I would have even been okay with something magically happening to him between now and me going home. If I knew where I was, I would walk. On second thought, the pain I felt when my underwear and jeans touched my vagina let me know it wasn't a good idea. It felt like I had a balloon like lump between my legs that wouldn't allow me to walk straight. My jeans felt like sandpaper. I could barely walk but I tried to walk normal. I didn't want to let him know that he succeeded. With every step the friction from my jeans rubbing up against my skin made my knees want to buckle. Please just let me make it home, I thought to myself. I hoped everyone was asleep. I wouldn't be able to hold myself together if anyone saw me.

I got in the car making sure I didn't make eye contact. I wish I could stab him. Dru Hill- *The Love We Had*, flowed from the speakers and i couldn't stand to hear the words. I turned my head and looked out the window. TK was driving peacefully and smoking as he came to a red light. The car came to a halt and I got out without hesitation. "Just so you know, I hate you" I said as I closed the door.   I clenched my teeth as rage and confusion flowed through my veins. I walked away before he could respond. I felt used and disgusting. Luckily I was only a block away from home. Was this my walk of shame? I was in pain but I got there as soon as I could and went straight into the bathroom. As soon as I closed the door, all I could do was cry. A hard rush of sadness came over me. Trying not to make any alarming sounds, I turned on the water to muffle the noise.

My heart was racing as small sounds escaped. I wanted to cry for help. I needed a hug, someone to beat his ass, something. This feeling was becoming all too familiar. Why was this happening to me? Why now? I turned on the shower and took my clothes off. I looked down to assess my injuries. One side of my labia was swollen, red and sensitive to the touch. It was stretched and funny looking. He was absolutely right. He left his mark, this isn't something that will go away. How will I explain this to anyone? I didn't want anyone to ever see what this asshole did to me. How will I say what happened to me when that time comes? I let the water run all over my body. I crouched on the shower floor letting the water focus on my legs. It was slightly soothing. The water washed my tears away but they kept coming. I let out a large gasp. Suddenly there was a knock at the bathroom door. My heart dropped.